Contents

Water in Our World 4

Water in a Desert 6

Water in a Frozen Land 8

Washing Clothes 10

No Clean Water 12

Walking for Water 14

Digging a Well 16

Clean Water for Everyone 18

Turning Fog into Water 20

Map: Where in the World? 22

Glossary 23

Index, Learn More Online 24

Words shown in **bold** in the text are explained in the glossary.

All the places in this book are shown on the map on page 22.

Water in Our World

We need water to drink.

We use water for cooking.

My World
Your World

Everybody Needs Water

by Ellen Lawrence

Ruby Tuesday Books

Published in 2015 by Ruby Tuesday Books Ltd.

Editor: Mark J. Sachner
Designer: Emma Randall
Production: John Lingham

Photo credits:
Alamy: 7, 10–11, 12, 14–15, 22; Arctic Photo: 9, 22; Corbis: 5 (bottom),
13, 22; FLPA: 6, 22; FogQuest: 20 (bottom), 21, 22; Shutterstock: Cover
(Marie Havens), 2 (Marie Havens), 4, 5 (top left), 5 (top right: vinhdav),
8, 16–17 (Gilles Paire), 18 (africa924), 19 (Pal Teravagimov), 20 (top),
22, 23 (Pal Teravagimov).

British Library Cataloguing In Publication Data (CIP)
is available for this title.

ISBN 978-1-910549-51-3

Printed in India

www.rubytuesdaybooks.com

**The picture on the front cover of this
book shows boys enjoying a bath
in small bowls of water. The boys
live in Uganda, in Africa.**

We wash our clothes with water.

We need water to keep clean.

We use water for keeping cool and having fun.

Water in a Desert

Many people live in places where it's hard to find water.

The San people live in the Kalahari Desert in Africa.

The San know many ways to find water in this hot, dry land.

One way is to drink rainwater that collects in small holes in trees.

This boy is using a straw made from a plant stem to drink rainwater.

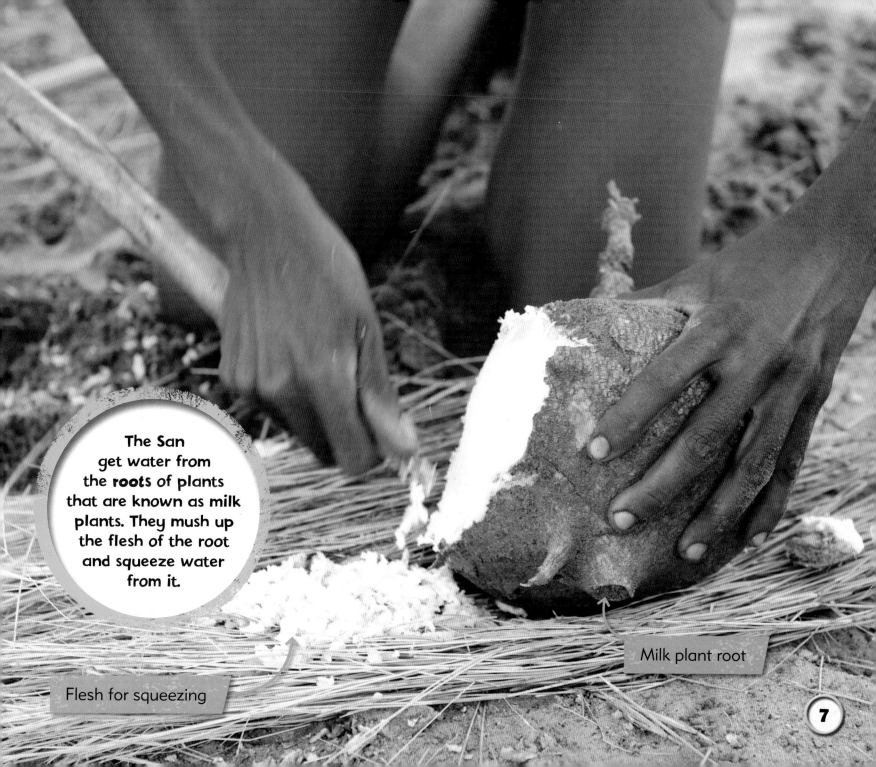

The San get water from the **roots** of plants that are known as milk plants. They mush up the flesh of the root and squeeze water from it.

Flesh for squeezing

Milk plant root

Water in a Frozen Land

The Nenets people live in Siberia in Russia.

It is so cold here that water in lakes and rivers freezes into solid ice.

Nenets people are reindeer **herders**. They live in small camps and move from place to place with their animals.

To get water, Nenets people collect snow.

Then they melt the snow over fires and cookers to make water for drinking and cooking.

A Nenets family collecting snow

Washing Clothes

Many people around the world wash their clothes in rivers and streams.

These women and girls in Ecuador are doing their families' washing.

To remove water from wet clothes, people hit them hard against rocks.

The freshly washed clothes are hung outdoors to dry in the sun.

No Clean Water

Millions of people get their drinking water from dirty streams and waterholes, or **polluted** rivers.

Dirty water can contain germs that give people **diarrhea** and other illnesses.

Every day, about 4000 children die because dirty water has made them ill.

In India, millions of people in cities have no water in their homes. Each day, people wait with cans and buckets for trucks to bring them water. Sometimes, the water is dirty.

Walking for Water

Every day, many children around the world must collect water for their families.

Some children have to walk for an hour or more to reach a waterhole, pond or stream.

Then they walk an hour back to home carrying a heavy can of water.

Many children have to make this journey three or four times each day!

A waterhole

In many families, it is the girls' job to collect water. They have no time to go to school or play with their friends.

These girls are collecting water in Uganda, in Africa.

Digging a Well

If a village has a well, people no longer have to spend hours collecting water.

Sometimes, **charities** help poor villages raise money to build a well.

Then **engineers** visit the village and choose a spot with water underground.

They drill into the ground and put pipes down into the water.

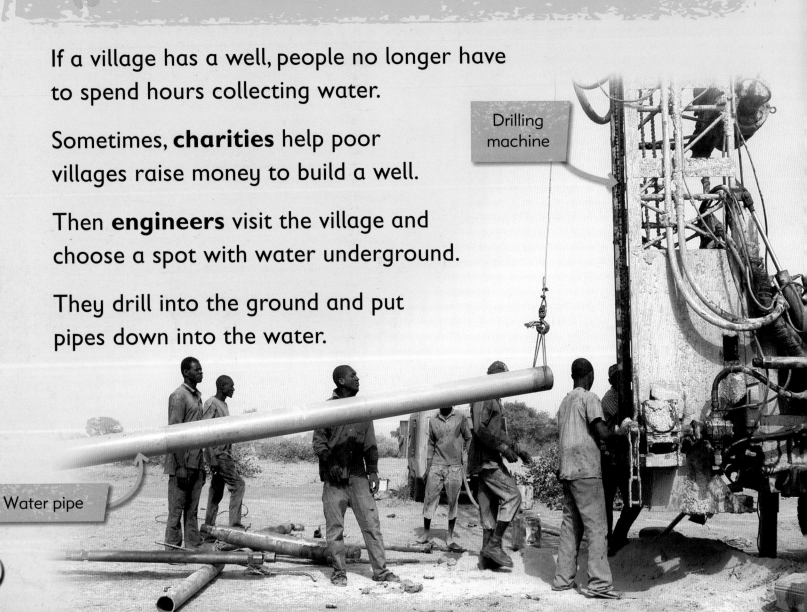

Drilling machine

Water pipe

Pipes carry water from deep underground to a pump on the surface. When people push the handle of the pump up and down, clean, fresh water pours out!

17

Clean Water for Everyone

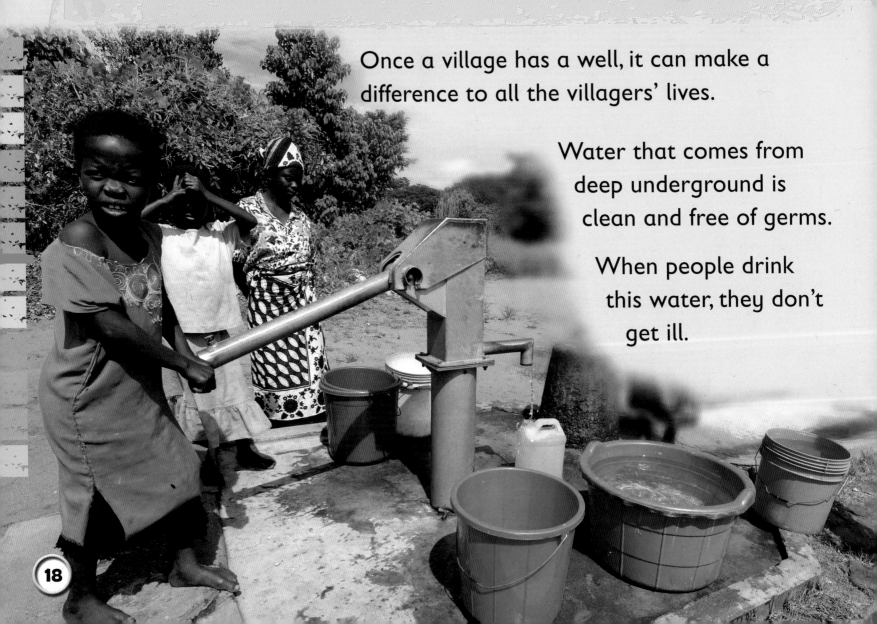

Once a village has a well, it can make a difference to all the villagers' lives.

Water that comes from deep underground is clean and free of germs.

When people drink this water, they don't get ill.

Having plenty of water makes it easier to grow vegetables and other crops.

Having clean water and better food makes everyone healthier.

If children don't have to spend hours collecting water, they have time to go to school.

Having water for hand washing stops germs spreading, too.

19

Turning Fog into Water

Some people live in places with little running water, but lots of fog.

Fog is made up of tiny drops of water.

Fog on a hillside

A fog collector

People collect fog using a fog collector made of mesh, or net.

The tiny drops of water in fog collect on the mesh.

These fog collectors supply water to a village in Guatemala.

Then the water from the fog collector runs into pipes and can be used for drinking, cooking and washing.

21

Where in the World?

United States
Page 4

Burkina Faso
Pages 12 and 16–17

United Kingdom
Page 5

Uganda
Cover and pages 14–15

Siberia, Russia
Pages 8–9

India
Pages 11 and 13

North America

Europe

Asia

Vietnam
Page 5

Africa

Guatemala
Pages 20–21

South America

Australia

Malawi
Page 18

Indonesia
Page 11

Ecuador
Page 10

Namibia
Page 4

South Africa
Pages 6–7

Swaziland
Page 19

Australia
Page 5

Glossary

charity
An organisation that raises money and uses it to do good work such as helping people living in poverty.

diarrhea
A stomach illness that makes people's stomach ache and their poo become liquid.

engineer
A person who uses maths, science and technology to design and build machines.

herder
A person who herds, or moves, animals from place to place so that the animals can find food.

polluted
Made dirty and often dangerous with pollution such as rubbish, oil, chemicals or even animal or human waste.

roots
Underground parts of a plant that take in water from soil. Some plants have long, thin roots. Others, such as milk plants, have fat, fleshy roots.

Index

C
charities 16
collecting water 13,
   14–15, 16, 19

D
deserts 6
diarrhea 12
dirty water 12

F
fog 20–21

G
germs (in water) 12,
   18–19

I
ice 8

N
Nenets people 8–9

P
pumps 17

S
San people 6–7
snow 9

W
washing and keeping
   clean 5, 19
washing clothes 5,
   10–11
wells 16–17, 18

Learn More Online

To learn more about water in our
everyday lives, go to
www.rubytuesdaybooks.com/water

24